This yearbook belongs to...

Kacde

Esme x

Hello and welcome to my 2023 yearbook — I really hope you enjoy it!

This Esme
Yearbook

Published by DJ Murphy (Publishers) Ltd, Olive Studio, Grange Road, Farnham, Surrey GU10 2DQ

WHO DID WHAT IN THIS ESME YEARBOOK 2023
Esme Higgs
Contributors Sarah Burgess, Louise Kittle, Nicky Moffatt, Bethany Searby
Head of Art and Design Sarah Garland
Design Jake Booth, James Kratz, Paul Smail, Adam Witt
Lifestyle photographers David Higgs, Lucy Merrell, Peter Nixon, @eventsthroughalens
Managing Director Zoe Cannon
Commercial Director Abi Cannon

This Esme Yearbook is produced under license by DJ Murphy (Publishers) Ltd.
© Copyright DJ Murphy (Publishers) Ltd.

Printed by Graphicom via dell'Industria – 36100 Vicenza, Italy

ISBN 978-1-913787-11-0

MIX
Paper from responsible sources
FSC® C013123

RRP £12.99

@THIS_ESME

JUST UPLOADED A NEW VIDEO

I have had sooo much fun this last year. I've trained harder than ever, I've met some amazing new friends and I've done stuff I couldn't have imagined. Here's a quick roundup!

Just getting started

Something I've been wanting to do for a really long time is a series of videos to help people start riding. I'm so passionate about horses and I want anyone and everyone who has an interest in horses to be able to give riding a go. I had a brilliant day working with Team Tutsham – riding school of the year 2021 – mucking in with the stable chores and finding out more about how they help all sorts of people start their riding journey.

Doing it myself

If you're an avid watcher of my channel you'll know how many hours I spent sanding, painting, and cleaning the yard as it transformed from a small garden set up to the yard of my dreams. There's now space for Duke, my ever-growing collection of saddle pads, and of course the scene of many a cleaning video – the wash bay! I literally can't tell you how hard I worked to make this transformation happen, but I am *sooo* pleased with the results!

Sky's the limit

While filming with Breen Equestrian I had no idea there was the most amazing treat lined up for me. They didn't just let me ride one of their international superstar horses – they let me jump him, too! Never have I felt so terrified and strangely confident at the same time as I approached some seriously massive fences on a horse I'd literally just met. Needless to say, Grand Prix horse, Duggie, was a total gem and I had the time of my life!

GCT Miami

Making the most of the relaxation of travel restrictions I headed to Miami for its leg of the Longines Global Champions Tour. This is the showjumping series that takes the best of the best to some of the most amazing places in the world. I can honestly say it doesn't get much better than Miami where the action literally takes place on the beach! With waves crashing in the background and crowds of sun seekers and surfers cheering on the horses, it's one of the most incredible shows I've ever been to.

Horsin' around

As horse shows up and down the country got back underway in 2021, I headed to Blenheim Horse Trials for the very first time. It's such a beautiful palace and the grounds are simply incredible. I loved watching the CCI-S 4* eight and nine year olds class in particular as there are sure to be some future Olympic horses in the field. Plus, I got to do some shopping and hang out with Radio 1's Greg James and Chris Smith!

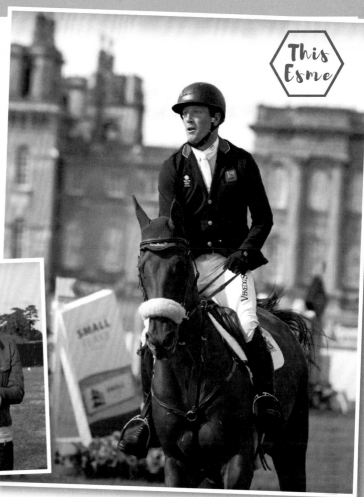

The fast and the furious

One of the challenges I enjoyed filming the most this year was horseball. You guys know me, I'm up for pretty much anything but this was next-level in terms of how quick the game is. The way the horses instinctively know where you need them to be made me believe they think they're playing too – and are desperate for the win! I made some awesome friends that day and I'm sure it won't be the last time I play horseball.

Big Day Out

It was so nice to see so many of you at PONY Magazine's Big Day Out. It had taken nearly two years for the event to finally happen, but it was definitely worth the wait. As well as meeting you guys, I watched the show, had a sneaky cuddle with Teddy the Shetland and hung out with Pony Nuts. I was totally mesmerised by the vaulting team's display, too – so much so that you can see what happened when I gave it a try for myself on page 44.

PERFECT MATCH

Rehoming Duke has honestly been one of the most incredible things I've ever done

About Duke

At just one day old, Duke was found abandoned. Without his mum to care for him, he wouldn't have survived. Fortunately, Duke was rescued by World Horse Welfare who hand reared him and made sure he had all the care he needed to survive and thrive. When I rehomed Duke he was just a yearling and ready to leave the World Horse Welfare farm he'd grown up on and become part of my herd. »

This Esme

" I can't bear to think what would have happened to Duke if he hadn't been rescued by World Horse Welfare. He's becoming such a confident and happy little pony — with more than his fair share of cheekiness! "

> Every night when I put the horses to bed I take Duke to say good night to all the others before he goes into his stable. It honestly melts my heart how much he loves Joey, Mickey and Casper.

Welcoming a new pony

There were lots of reasons I wanted to rehome a pony. Mickey's health conditions mean he needs to be on restricted grass, particularly through the summer months, and so he's no longer a good field buddy for Casper and Joey, who enjoy having plenty of grass to munch on. I could see that Mickey needed a companion to keep him company, offer him friendship and be someone to play with.

It made total sense to me to look at rehoming a pony from a charity as my first option, because it helps to free up vital places at the charity's farm for horses in desperate need of rescuing. Because the new pony was primarily going to be a companion for Mickey, it didn't matter to me whether he or she could be ridden or not, or if they were too small for me to ride. It was important that they were a native type so that they would have similar dietary requirements to Mickey – or the dynamic wouldn't work. I also wanted a horse or pony I felt a genuine connection with. The horses are my life and a huge part of the family so any horse I was looking to rehome had to get on with everyone.

> Duke is 100% part of the family. When I'm travelling for work my mum's the first to volunteer to look after him – she loves leaving little treats for him to find!

The process

There are lots of charities which rehome horses and ponies who have come into their care. Most list the horses that are ready to find a new home on their website and clearly explain what the horse can and can't do, plus any issues he may have. If you find a horse or pony that suits what you're looking for and you have the permission of your parent or guardian you can start the application process. The team that deal with rehoming at your chosen charity will review your application and get back to you. If they think you might be a suitable match you'll be invited to meet the horse.

On your visit you may be asked to groom or handle the horse so that the rehoming team can assess how competent you are on the ground. If the horse or pony you're looking at rehoming is ridden, they will also look at your riding ability to make sure you'll be a good fit for each other. If everything goes well and you both think you've found the right match, someone from the charity will visit the place where you intend to keep your adopted horse. They'll assess if it's suitable for the needs of the horse or pony you're considering rehoming and suggest any changes which need to be made.

Before you can take your new pony home they will have one last vet check and your parent or guardian will need to sign a rehoming agreement. It's normal for the horse or pony to remain the property of the charity – this protects the horse from being sold or ending up in a bad situation again. Lots of charities charge a rehoming fee which is generally a small amount of money which goes straight back into the charity to help the next pony that needs them.

The benefits of rehoming a horse

- When you rehome a horse from a charity, like World Horse Welfare, experts will have carefully assessed him in all kinds of situations and they'll tell you honestly what he's like. They won't tell you he's capable of doing something he can't or exaggerate, and they'll give you advice on any special care he may need
- Your relationship with the charity doesn't stop the moment you put the horse on the trailer. They'll be there to offer advice and support whenever you need it and will check in with you from time to time to see how everything's going
- Giving a horse or pony a second chance is so rewarding. I feel proud that my family and I are giving Duke such a happy life after he had such a difficult start

POLE

PREPARATION

Before I tackle any polework exercises, my horses need a good warm-up workout

Getting started

Polework can be super-strenuous on your pony, so before you start it's mega important to give him a great warm-up. I like to allow both of my horses, in this case Casper, time to chill-out on a long rein in walk when I first enter the arena so they can take in the surroundings. Even when we're just walking on a long rein, I like to make sure they're marching on with a nice forward, active walk – not dawdling around without making any effort.

Hot to trot

Once I feel as though Casper's ready to pick up the pace, I gather the reins and ask him forward with my leg into a working trot. Fairly quickly I like to ride transitions within the pace, asking for five or six collected strides and then a few longer ones here and there to make sure he's listening to me and that I have an adjustable trot. This is essential for polework because your pony needs to be able to shorten or lengthen his stride in order to accommodate the poles once you get started.

It's important to ride evenly on both reins, so once I've completed a few circles in one direction, I change the rein and mix things up with a transition to walk for three strides as I cross the centre line. I ride the same exercise on the other rein, trying to feel whether Casper's responding when I ask for collection and lengthening.

Casper completely loves polework

Top tip

Polework's actually really hard work for horses, so make sure you take plenty of breaks and keep your sessions short and positive.

Calm collected canters

When I think about what sort of canter I want for polework, I imagine my jumping canter – it has lots of energy, bounce and is really adjustable. It also needs to feel balanced and as though I'm being taken forward. This is exactly the sort of canter I want for polework, too. I pick up canter and then ride a diamond shape (instead of a circle) so that I can check Casper's listening to my outside leg as I make each turn and feel if he's really coming through from behind and working over his back. I do this a few times on each rein and ride a simple transition through trot each time I change direction. Now I'm ready to tackle some poles!

This canter needs more oomph!

Poles apart

If you want to have a go at some of the polework exercises I enjoy riding with my horses, you can adapt them to fit your pony's stride length. Here's a rough guide to trot pole distances, but if your pony's particularly long- or short-striding you may need to go up or down a distance. If you're not sure, it's best to ask your instructor for help.

12.2hh	approximately 110cm apart
13.2hh	approximately 115cm apart
14.2hh	approximately 120cm apart
15.2hh	approximately 140cm apart
16.2hh	approximately 160cm apart

RAY OF LIGHT

Celebrate the spring equinox – and the extra hours of daylight – with this super-fab fan of poles

Top tip

If I want to really test Casper I alternate between the inside and the outside of the poles to shorten and lengthen his stride.

THE SET UP

What you'll need: 7 or 8 poles
The arrangement: Place the poles in a semi-circle so the inside edges of the poles are approximately 60cm apart, the middle sections are approximately 120cm apart and the outer edges are around 180cm apart. If the pony you're riding is much bigger or smaller than Casper you'll need to increase or decrease the gaps between the poles to better match his stride length.

THE AIM

I love this exercise and find it really helps my flatwork. The idea of the fan is that when you ride through the centre of each pole, the distance between poles will be your pony's normal working trot. As you ride the outer edge of the poles he'll need to lengthen his frame and extend his stride to make the increased distance between each one. When you tackle the inside edge of the poles, your pony will need to collect his trot and take higher, shorter steps. So, with one nifty set up I can work Casper and Joey through their paces and make sure I can move them on and collect them back within trot.

THE LONG & THE SHORT OF IT

Once Casper's happy trotting through the centre of the poles it's time to mix it up a bit! I know that he really likes to power on in a big trot, but before I do this, I ask him to collect a little and take shorter steps, keeping the same level of energy. It's so important that I have in my mind that I don't actually want Casper to go slower. What I'm aiming for is a more animated trot, with lots of energy and more lift than his normal working trot. When we're both ready, I approach the inside of the fan where the poles are closer together. This helps Casper to collect his stride even more. I do these two or three times on each rein before giving him a big pat and a breather.

When it comes to asking for some longer strides, Casper can become excited and try to canter. The poles are really good for this as the rhythm of stepping over one pole and then another helps to keep him focused and asks him to lengthen through his frame so that he can reach the bigger distance between them. When we're both ready I approach the outer edge of the poles in a forward trot and keep my leg on as we ride through them. I concentrate on rising higher so that I stay in balance with Casper's longer trot strides and also allowing with my hand so that he can stretch through his whole frame as he goes over the poles. Again, it's important to do this exercise on each rein to make sure he's working evenly through his body.

GETTING STARTED

After completing my polework warm up I approach the very centre of the fan with Casper. While it's tempting to glance down at the poles, it's important that I look up and around the semi-circle so that my weight is in the right place and Casper knows where we're going. I use my inside rein to ask for the bend and my outside leg to guide him through the turn so that we stay on the right line. As we go over them, I try to stay soft with my hands and allow Casper to use his body to step up and over each pole. There's a lot to think about, so before we add any complexity, I ride this line a few times on each rein.

"Having dyslexia means I tend to think in pictures rather than words — which is probably one of the reasons I do what I do for a living!"

5 THINGS YOU DIDN'T KNOW ABOUT ME!

As an equestrian vlogger I share a lot about myself with you guys, but here are some things you might not have heard...

1 Bonkers about bouldering

When I'm not riding or working, I really enjoy bouldering. Not only is it good for core body strength and balance, but you have to be pretty flexible, too. Luckily I'm not scared of heights!

2 Serious about sunscreen

Despite not wearing much make up, I literally don't go out without putting on sunscreen. I have naturally pale skin so I'm very conscious of the damage that can be done by being out in the sun. You'll often find me in a baseball cap, too, which helps to keep the sun out of my eyes and off my face.

3 Team Casper

In the early days of owning Casper, he was quite tricky to say the least! I fell off all the time and one day he even bucked my instructor off. My parents were pretty worried, so suggested I sell Casper and even offered to give me additional money to buy a horse who wouldn't keep bucking me off. Instead, I asked them to put that money towards an arena which would mean I could ride Casper a lot more and hopefully it would calm him down – so I didn't keep ending up on the floor. It worked and now he's a total superstar!

4 Dealing with Dyslexia

When I was at school I was diagnosed with dyslexia which means I have some difficulty reading. I'm passionate about making the written word accessible to people who have dyslexia. So, when I'm working on projects like this yearbook, I always ask the designers to use dyslexia-friendly fonts as much as possible so that everyone can enjoy my books.

5 Mickey-mad!

Did you see the super-cute poster of Mickey and Duke in PONY magazine? Well I bet you didn't expect it to be pride of place in my kitchen! The issue came out while I was in South Africa and when I got home and stepped inside the front door all I could see was the most enormous picture of the boys hanging above the fridge. My mum adores the ponies as much as I do and just couldn't resist putting it up for all to see!

HAVE A GO AT...
POLOCROSSE

This sport is definitely a lot harder than it looks, but I had so much fun getting to grips with polocrosse!

The aim of the game

Polocrosse is a fast-paced mix of polo and lacrosse, and is one of the most exciting equestrian disciplines. Teams of six players face off against one another and each player carries a racquet with a net for them to catch, carry and throw the sponge rubber ball – and hopefully score a goal!

Ball skills

Picking up the ball from the floor is one of the most important skills needed for polocrosse because you certainly don't want to be getting off your horse every time you drop it! To do this you scrape the ball up in your net with an upwards motion, then flick your wrist over and back to stop the ball from flying straight out of the net again. It took me *sooo* long to get the hang of this, but I got there in the end!

I spent a lot of time learning to throw and catch the ball before I even got on a pony – it's probably just as well because my aim wasn't the best to begin with! For some reason my catching was actually pretty good, but when it came to throwing I really struggled with the over arm throw.

Tackling was the final skill I needed to learn. Using the side of the racquet, the aim is to hit the bottom of the ball while it's in your opponent's net, knocking it high into the air so that you can catch it.

One of my more successful throws!

Riding skills

You need a basic level of riding ability before you can have a go at polocrosse. A secure seat is a must because you need to be comfortable reaching to either side of the horse with your racquet to throw and catch the ball, leaning right down when you need to pick up the ball and turning at speed. Instead of using two hands on the reins, you hold both reins in one hand and use them to neck rein, just as you would in western riding. This leaves your other hand free to hold the racquet. Whenever you're carrying the ball you must hold the racquet on the right-hand side of the horse if you're right handed and the left-hand side of the horse if you're left handed. You're allowed to reach across to the other side of the horse when you need to pick up, catch or throw the ball.

As well as tackling, you can defend by riding off against another rider. This is when you use your horse to ride alongside the other horse and push them off their line so that they can't take a shot at goal. However, you are not allowed to elbow another rider, stop your horse over the ball or cross in front of another horse, because this would be dangerous. »

Did you know?
The ball used in polocrosse is made from sponge so it doesn't hurt the horses if it accidentally hits them.

The get up

South African stock saddles are often used for top level polocrosse because they're lightweight and give the players lots of support as they reach for the ball. The horses often wear a standing martingale because the riders only ever have one hand on the reins so it helps to keep the horses under control during the tight turns and quick, stop-start nature of the game. No matter what level you ride at, your horse will need to wear bandages or sports boots as well as overreach boots on all four feet.

The game

Each team is made up of six players, but only three are on the pitch at once. Players take turns to play chukkas, which last eight minutes, and there are usually six or eight chukkas in a game. There are three positions:

- No. 1 – Attack
- No. 2 – Centre
- No. 3 – Defence

The position you play in will determine which areas of the pitch you're allowed to ride in. Everyone is allowed in the middle area, but only the attacking No. 1 player and opposition No. 3 player can go into each goal-scoring area.

Players pick up or catch the ball and pass to one another until their team's No. 1 has the ball in their goal-scoring area and can take a shot at goal. You can't ride with the ball into the penalty area. Instead you must either bounce and re-catch the ball once you're over the line, or pass to the No. 1 player in the penalty area.

The game begins with opponents standing in pairs side-by-side in the centre area, with the No. 1 players at the front and the No. 3 players at the back. The ball is thrown in over their heads and the players have the chance to catch it. If no one catches the ball players turn their horses 180° to the outside before charging after the ball.

Staying cool under pressure!

Practise pays off!

Field diagram labels: 27.5m, 91.5m, 2.5m, 10m, penalty line, centre area, penalty line, 55m, goal scoring area, 7m, goal scoring area, 12m, run off, 3m, 146.5m

Did you know?
Polocrosse racquets are made from bamboo, so they're pretty flexible.

Sometimes I think
Casper knows me better
than I know myself

SPRING HAIR!

Duke loves a pamper sesh, but at this time of year I get a whole lot more than I bargained for!

Why do horses shed their coats?

Horses and ponies shed their coats in spring and autumn as they prepare for the warmer and colder months. However, it's not the temperature that controls when their coat changes – but the hours of daylight. In the UK, from the end of August when the days are getting shorter, light receptors in horses' eyes send a message to their brain which releases hormones that cause them to shed their summer coats and start to grow thicker winter ones. Come February, when the days get longer, horses prepare for the warmer weather by shedding their winter fluff and growing new, slick summer coats.

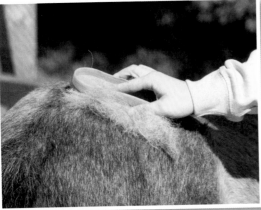

Little and often

The moulting process can go on for weeks, depending on the weather. Duke first started losing some of his winter coat at the beginning of March. Then his moulting seemed to go on pause for a bit, but by the middle of April he was in full flow again! By grooming Duke a little bit each day, I can stay on top of his hair loss so he doesn't get all itchy. Mickey lends a hand, too, by grooming Duke with his teeth when they're out in the field together.

My favourite tools for the job

There are so many products on the market designed to deal with moulting. From good old-fashioned rubber curry combs to shedding blades and even special mitts you can wear to stroke the hair away. I quite like to use a magic brush – it's quick and easy, plus Duke seems to think he's getting a massage at the same time!

Sharing is caring

One thing you may not know about the yard is that my mum loves feeding the wild birds. It's got to the point where many of them have names, like Colin the crow, who spends most of his days attacking his reflection in the trailer mirrors as he desperately tries to defend his territory against, well... himself! Anyway, something I love to do in the spring when the horses are moulting is leave some of their coat hair out for the birds to line their nests with. This year Duke's coat has been a real hit with all our feathered friends!

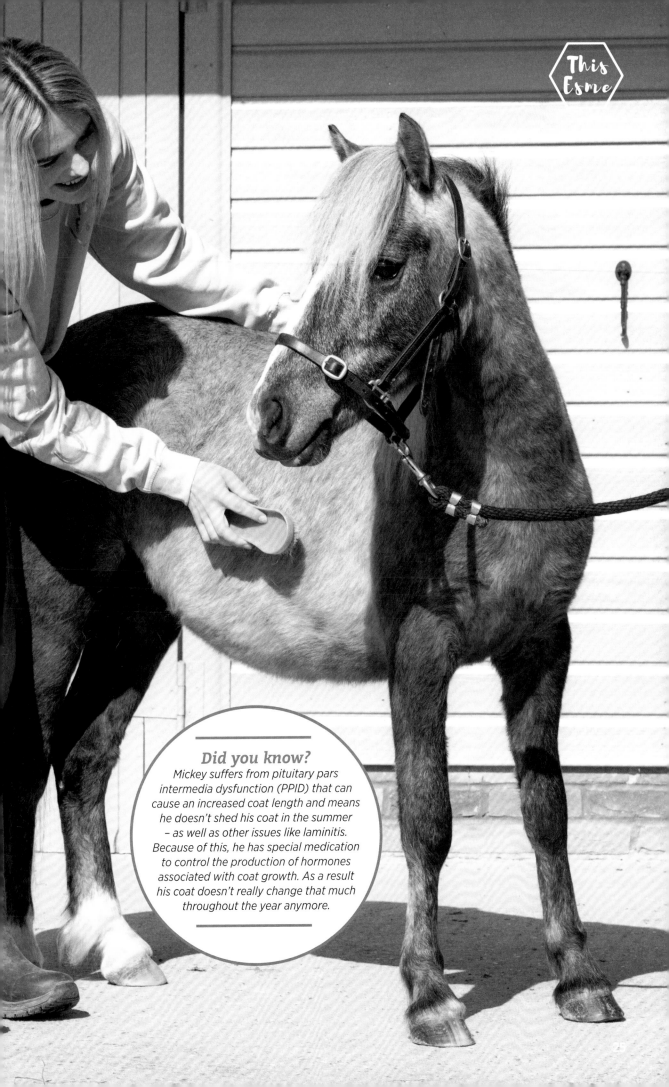

Did you know?

Mickey suffers from pituitary pars intermedia dysfunction (PPID) that can cause an increased coat length and means he doesn't shed his coat in the summer – as well as other issues like laminitis. Because of this, he has special medication to control the production of hormones associated with coat growth. As a result his coat doesn't really change that much throughout the year anymore.

If you plan to ride a dressage test with your pony, no matter what level you're aiming for, you'll need to ride a centre line at the start and finish – so it's an essential movement to master. Bizarrely, Joey loves strutting his stuff down the centre line. It's as though he knows something important is about to happen and he really tries to do his best for me!

26

Preparation is key

Before I even start to make a turn onto the centre line I need to prepare Joey for what's coming up. Turning onto the centre line is like riding a quarter of a circle from the track onto the centre line. Because Joey is still fairly inexperienced at dressage, I ride a quarter of a 10-metre circle. This means I need to leave the track halfway between the long side and the centre line and aim to reach the centre line one metre before the imaginary marker D – check out the diagram below if you're not sure where that is!

As I ride down the long side of the school, I keep an eye on the point at which I need to start my turn. I signal to Joey that I'm about to ask him to do something by giving him a little half-halt as we head past the F or K marker. Then, just as I'm about to reach the point where I need to start our turn, I switch my gaze to the C marker and ride my turn onto the centre line using my outside leg to guide Joey around the turn and my inside rein to ask for a little bend. By the time we're passing the D marker we should be heading straight towards C. It can take a bit of practise to make sure you hit the centre line without over or undershooting, but once you've got your eye in you can master the turn.

Did you know?
Riders with more experienced horses are able to ride a quarter of a six metre circle onto the centre line, which gives a neater turn.

Super straight

Once you've made it onto the centre line it's all about straightness. I find that it helps to ride Joey forward – if he's dawdling along, we tend to wobble from one side to the other. I look directly to where I imagine the judge is sitting and try to keep my shoulders and hips square to the centre line to help Joey stay straight. Ideally the judge only wants to see his front legs – if his bottom is poking out one side or the other, he's not completely straight!

> When I'm going down the centre line for real at a competition I try to smile at the judge, too!

All square

At the end of a dressage test you will need to ride a transition to halt. This is the last chance you have to impress the judge, so it's worth giving it your all. Again, I find that preparation is key and I prepare Joey with a half-halt so that he knows I'm going to ask him to do something. I try to visualise it in my head as a step forward into the halt. This prevents us from collapsing in a heap with Joey on his forehand, and makes sure I ride forward in the transition so that he steps into a square halt with his hind legs directly behind his front legs.

FIRST AID BOX TOUR

Find out what essentials I keep close to hand just in case of an emergency

Hibiscrub

This antimicrobial skin cleanser helps to prevent infections by killing germs on the skin. You might have seen this in hospitals or at your local GP surgery as it's used on humans, too. It's my absolute go-to if the horses have a small cut or signs of mud fever that need a good antibacterial wash. Dilute it as per the instructions and rinse well.

Cotton wool

Used for cleansing and padding wounds. For dressings, the cotton wool goes between the dressing and bandage to avoid pressure points. Never put cotton wool directly on a wound.

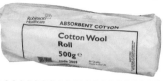

Oral syringe

This type of syringe is handy to keep in my first aid box in case one of the horses is prescribed a medicine they're not keen on eating. Just as if I was giving my horse a wormer, I pop the syringe in the side of the horse's mouth and squirt the medication in, so I know they're getting the right dose.

Tape

This vet tape is a real must have item! If I'm applying a hoof poultice because of an abscess or to protect the hoof if one of the horses has lost a shoe, I use this to keep the vet wrap in place and stop the dressing becoming wet in the stable.

Hoof poultice

One of the most common causes of lameness in horses is foot abscesses. Your vet or farrier will be able to confirm a suspected abscess, and trim away the hoof to help it drain if needed. A poultice helps to drain an abscess, and can prevent dirt getting into it, too. I soak the poultice in warm water and apply directly to the hoof using vet wrap to secure it in place.

Thermometer

A horse's temperature should be 37.2–38.5°. If I think one of the equines is a bit off colour, one of the first things I do is take their temperature. When I speak to the vet about them, being able to let them know the horse's temperature tells the vet how serious the situation might be.

Vet wrap

This brightly coloured bandage is elasticated and cohesive, so it holds wound dressings in place without affecting the horse's circulation. I use them when I need to poultice a hoof or if one of the horses has a cut that needs dressing.

Absorbent dressing

These dressings are designed to cover a wound. They promote healing and will absorb any discharge from the wound.

Gamgee

This is a special fabric that has a layer of high quality absorbent cotton wool sandwiched between two cotton gauze covers. It's ideal as a secondary dressing to cushion and protect the wound. Gamgee can also be used as a swab to clean wounds, too.

Top tip
It's really helpful to have a fully kitted out first aid kit to help you treat minor injuries – but you should always call a vet if you're worried about a horse or pony.

FIRST AID

DREAM BARNS

I'm not going to lie – I love a good tack room, but some of these facilities are simply out of this world!

RETRO BARN

Way back in 2017 I did my first-ever tack room tour. I'd only been running my channel for a couple of years and it was the most requested video from you guys. I was so excited to share it with you. It had everything I'd ever dreamed of – a sink, shelves, drawers for my horse boots and bonnets, and hanging space for my ever-growing saddle pad collection!

FANTASTIC FACILITIES

The amazing set up at Forest Oaks Equestrian has everything you and your pony could ever wish for – from the covered horse walker to the amazing arenas.

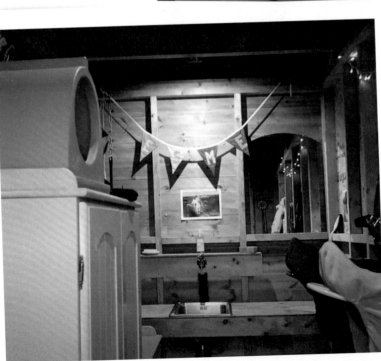

GOING STATE SIDE

When I went on tour to the USA in 2019, I discovered a whole new level when it came to beautiful tack rooms. I hadn't seen anything like it before and I was completely blown away by the beautiful storage solutions, lighting, and how organised they were. Over the past few years it seems we've learnt a lot from our US equestrian friends!

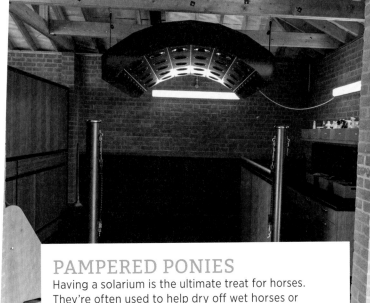

PAMPERED PONIES

Having a solarium is the ultimate treat for horses. They're often used to help dry off wet horses or warm up their back muscles before exercise. Now that I'm lucky enough to have my own at home I can categorically say Joey loves it! »

NEXT LEVEL ORGANISATION

I just love how this tack room uses every little bit of space to store everything you could possibly need for your horse – and it's all in one place. A tack room with a ladder is a definite life goal!

ALL ABOUT THE DETAILS

It really is the little things that set apart the most beautiful facilities. I love these plaques and engraved brass details!

LIGHT AND AIRY

These barn-style fronts on outdoor stables give the horses so much natural light and airflow that I simply fell in love with them!

A ROOM WITH A VIEW

When you step inside this incredible arena at Ellie McCarthy's yard, you feel inspired to be the dressage rider you never knew you could be. The skylight and huge windows, as well as full mirrors, make this indoor feel like you're outside – without the risk of getting soaked!

THE YARD MASCOT!

No top yard's complete without it's own troublesome Shetland! Duke's actually a Welsh Mountain pony, but he definitely fits the bill of having an enormous personality trapped inside a tiny physique!

ULTIMATE UPGRADE

Last year I was lucky enough to be able to extend my stable block to make room for Duke and also give my tack room a long overdue upgrade. My collection of riding helmets, boots, bonnets and pads had well and truly outgrown my original tack room, so I was able to incorporate all the fantastic features I'd seen when visiting amazing yards into my own dream space.

SUMMER
CARE ROUTINE

We all love a bit of sunshine, but at this time of year I need to take extra special care of one particular equine!

Less is more

The saying 'the grass is always greener' is literally true for poor Mickey who has his grazing restricted in the spring and summer to prevent him from getting laminitis. Horses and ponies like Mickey who suffer from PPID are more likely to develop laminitis than other equines, so I have to be super strict with him and make sure he doesn't have too much lush green grass by fencing off a small paddock for him and Duke.

Sun cream

Horses and ponies can get sunburnt just like you and me. Mickey's particularly sensitive to the sun because he has pink skin around his eyes and muzzle due to his cremello colouring. By putting on a high factor sun cream every day before he goes out in the field I can help to protect him – he's not always the biggest fan of me applying it, though!

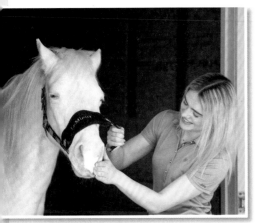

Buzz off

Midges, black flies, horse flies and stable flies, to name just a few, can be the bane of a horse's life during the summer months – making him irritable and itchy. I try to keep the flies away from the horses as much as possible by regularly poo picking the fields and turning the horses out at night so that they can come into the shelter of their stables during the day, when flies are at their most active. I also like to use fly rugs and masks to keep the flies at bay. Zebra rugs are said to confuse flies so they don't know where to land. They're also light and breathable, which prevents the horses from overheating in the hot weather.

This Esme

Mickey blue-eyes

Being a cremello with two blue eyes means Mickey is much more sensitive to light than other horses. You'll often see him blinking in bright sunlight as it makes his eyes sore. Wearing a fly mask can help Mickey by filtering out some of the natural daylight and keeping him more comfortable.

Beat the heat

On super-hot days I like to give the horses a cooling wash down to make them feel more comfortable. Mickey really enjoys this as his coat can make him a bit hot and sweaty. He also loves it when I treat him to an ice treat like the ones I made on page 36.

MAKE A HORSEY
ICE LICK

Mickey absolutely loves cooling down with these super-chilled treats

What you'll need:
- apples
- carrots
- sharp knife
- freezer-safe container
- water

1 Chop your apples so that they're a suitable size for a horse or pony to eat. I normally cut mine into eight by cutting the apple straight through its core, then cutting each half into four.

2 Now cut the carrots into small, rectangular pieces. It's important to always cut carrots lengthways as horses and ponies can choke on round chunks.

3 Pop your chopped fruit and vegetables into the container and fill it with water, leaving a little bit of room for the water to expand as it freezes.

Top tip
You could use other fruit and vegetables in your lick – just make sure they're safe for ponies to eat. Casper loves swede and Duke's a big fan of blackberries!

4 Place in the freezer overnight or until the whole thing is completely frozen.

5 Take your ice lick from the freezer and leave for a few minutes – this will make it easier to remove from the container. Then tip it onto the floor for your fave pony to enjoy!

"On a hot summer's day there's nothing Mickey likes more than these tasty treats!"

BABY STEPS

Duke has such a cheeky and curious nature that he's really enjoying getting to grips with a little bit of groundwork

Even though Duke won't ever be big enough for me to ride, it's important that he has a good basic education. Doing groundwork with him helps to boost our bond and makes sure Duke knows I'm in charge. This is really important with a hand-reared horse, like Duke, because the boundaries can easily become blurred!

STAND

It sounds silly, but one of the first things I taught Duke is to stand still when I ask him to. This is a life skill he'll carry with him whatever he does as he grows up. Horses need to stand for the vet, the farrier, at road crossings and in all sorts of different situations – so it's worth putting the time in to make sure he understands what's being asked of him. When I'm ready for him to stop I use my voice to gently ask him to 'stand'. Once he's stationary I give him lots of praise.

The next step is for me to be able to step away from Duke while he stays rooted to the spot. He finds this hard at the moment, but with patience and time he'll soon understand what he needs to do.

BACK UP

Teaching Duke to step backwards when I ask him to is an important part of him learning about personal space. When Duke's worried about something he likes to cling to my side, but it's important he respects the boundaries of what is my personal space and what is his. Even though he's only small, he still weighs more than three times what I do – and it could really hurt if he were to run me over!

To ask Duke to move back I put my hand on his chest and apply a little pressure while I say 'back' clearly. Once he's taken two or three steps I praise him so he knows that he's done the right thing. Eventually, I should just be able to signal to him with my hand and he will move back. »

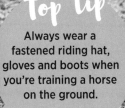

Top tip

Always wear a fastened riding hat, gloves and boots when you're training a horse on the ground.

MOVE SIDEWAYS

The next skill I'm teaching Duke is to move sideways away from pressure. This is a brilliant skill to teach horses who will one day be ridden, but even if they aren't, it's still useful to be able to position your horse where you want him. Just like the aid for backing up, I place my hand on Duke's side. As I apply some gentle pressure I say 'over' clearly. When he takes a step or two I'm really quick to praise him.

BETWEEN POLES

Horses are flight animals by nature, which means they want to run from things they think might eat them. Unfortunately lots of horses worry that all sorts of things you and I know are harmless may also turn into a scary monster. Because of this flight instinct, it can be a big ask to make a horse walk between two objects that are close together. I've started training Duke to walk between two poles – you can see in the photo that Duke isn't concerned about the pole on his left as I'm between him and it, but he has a watchful eye on the pole on his right, which might eat him at any moment!

I have positioned the poles quite far apart for the time being to give Duke plenty of room and reduce the amount of pressure he feels. Doing everything in a calm, confident manner lets Duke know that there's nothing to be scared of. After a few goes walking through the poles, Duke's feeling relaxed enough to stand between them. I keep our training sessions short as he's still young, so I'll wait until next time before repeating the exercise and then slowly reduce the gap between the poles.

Top tip

You don't need fancy equipment for desensitisation training. Whatever you can find will do so long as it's safe.

DESENSITISATION

Like most young horses, Duke hasn't seen much outside of his paddock, so when I'm working him in hand I include some desensitisation training. Today I introduced him to a rainbow filler, which he was quite unsure about. Because Duke seemed nervous of the filler, it was important that I let him touch and smell it so he could start to understand that he doesn't need to be afraid of it. As he becomes increasingly familiar with the filler and shows me that he's relaxed and not frightened, I'll ask him to walk beside it. Eventually I want to be able to walk one side of the filler while Duke walks the other – but this may take some time!

In this particular session we did some reinforcement training with an umbrella. It can be quite frightening for a horse to see a person out walking with an umbrella as it alters their silhouette and so sometimes the horse can't quite work out whether it's a person. Duke and I spent time over the winter working with umbrellas in the safety of the arena, so he could get used to them at his own pace. He was a little anxious to begin with, but quickly came round to the idea once I'd given him a few scratchies to help him relax. He's not phased by them any more, but we keep practising to keep up his confidence.

SCENIC SCHOOLING

You guys know I love a good blast when I'm out hacking, but did you know I also use the great outdoors for flatwork

Top tip

It can be harder to work both reins evenly when you're not in the arena – but try to do everything on each rein if you can.

" Schooling Casper out hacking really helps to hold his interest "

A SCHOOL WITH A VIEW

Going round in circles in the arena can feel a bit, well... boring! Casper, in particular, can quickly resort to potato mode when there aren't any jumps or poles to concentrate on so I like to spice things up by schooling in the open air while we're on a hack. I'm very lucky that there are a few local fields and open green spaces I can use for schooling, but even if your hacking routes are more confined to bridle paths there's still plenty you can do. Here's my top five exercises for schooling while out and about!

1. Forward and back

A great exercise you can do almost anywhere is to ride transitions within the pace. For example, I might ask Casper to travel in a collected walk for 20 strides then push him forward into a medium walk for 20 strides before coming back again to a more collected walk.

Try riding changes of pace in walk

2. Bend and flex

When we're trotting along a long straight track it's a great opportunity to practise some stretching with Casper. First I ask him to flex a little to the right and bend through his body in that direction while we move forwards for five or six strides. Next I straighten him up and make sure his ears, shoulders and hips are all facing forward for a few strides. Then I ask Casper to flex to the left for five or six steps before straightening up again.

3. Side to side

Casper isn't always the most keen to perform lateral movements in the school, but when I'm out in the open I ask him to take a few sideways steps in a leg-yield. On a wide track I ask Casper to look slightly to the left and use my left leg to ask him to move over to the right. Then I ride him straight for a couple of strides before asking him to look a little to the right and move away from my right leg to the other side of the track.

4. Perfect circles

When I come across a big open space I like to put my accuracy to the test by riding trot circles. On page 58 I explain how I ride perfect circles in the arena, but out in the open it's *sooo* much harder! I try to pick out some tufts of grass to aim for and then focus on keeping just the right amount of inside bend, being careful to not let Casper drift to the inside or outside.

5. All square

Every dressage test you'll ride ends with a transition to halt, so I like to ride one or two each time I'm in the saddle. Halt transitions are also great for making sure your pony's listening to you and to check he moves off your leg quickly when you ask. Instead of thinking about screeching to a stop, I try to visualise Casper stepping forward into the halt transition. When I use my leg to ask him forward into halt he's more likely to make a neat square one.

Perfect practise for dressage on grass

HAVE A GO AT...
VAULTING

I was super excited to try the art of vaulting, but soon discovered I'm not as flexible as I used to be!

What's it all about?
Often described as gymnastics on horseback, vaulting can be practised competitively or just for fun. At the higher levels, exercises are performed in canter but don't panic, beginner vaulters – like me – start in walk!

Vaulting's history

Believe it or not, vaulting's earliest roots date back 3,500 years. It has evolved along different paths – circus performers, trick riders and Roman riding, for example.

Vaulting as we know it today became an equestrian discipline in 1983, with the first World Championships taking place in Switzerland in 1986.

You feel so high up in the air when you're standing on a 17.1hh horse!

The get up

Guess what? Vaulting horses don't wear saddles! Instead, a shock-absorbing carbon fibre back pad with a gel pad underneath is used to keep them comfortable. The horse wears a snaffle bridle with side-reins attached to help keep him straight and balanced, and he's controlled via a lunge line by a person standing in the middle of a 15m circle.

A roller with handles attached to it – known as grips – and two leather straps called cossacks are used by the vaulter to help them perform the various exercises they have to do.

For training the vaulters wear standard gym kit of close-fitting leggings or tights and a top. Specialist vaulting shoes are available, but if you're just trying it out then ballet shoes or soft pumps are best. Competition outfits are really glamorous, with brightly coloured unitards.

The compulsory seven

In competitions, riders carry out a routine of exercises on horseback to music, with each movement scored from 0–10, just like a dressage test!

There are seven exercises that must be included in a competition routine:

1. Vault on

With the horse only wearing a roller, there's no option to mount in the conventional way. Instead, competitors must vault onto the horse, jumping on both feet and swinging their right leg up as high as possible, while their left leg hangs down. The aim is to land softly astride the horse's back, with the upper body vertical.

2. Basic seat

Here the vaulter's position is put to the test. Sitting on the horse as you would if you were riding normally, arms are held out to the side with hands raised until they're level with your ears. The rider's legs stay wrapped around the horse's body with toes pointing down – the opposite to riding with stirrups! This felt a bit weird to me at first, after years of riding with my toes slightly higher than my heels!

3. Flag

Slightly trickier, the vaulter must hop onto his or her knees, extending the right leg out behind them and stretching the left arm out in front at the same height as the right leg! ≫

45

4. Stand

Keeping both knees bent slightly, buttocks tucked forward and hands held out to the sides, the vaulter has to adopt a standing position for four horse's strides.

I'm not going to lie, it took a bit of convincing for me to stand up at speed!

5. Mill

Think round the world for this exercise. You bring your right leg over the neck so you're sitting on sideways, then the left leg swings over the horse's croup so you're sitting on backwards. Keep going until you're facing forward again.

6. Scissors

Here things get really difficult. The vaulter must swing into a handstand position then return to the horse's back facing backwards. Another swing of the legs and they're facing forwards again. In this exercise vaulters are penalised if they land heavily on the horse's back.

7. Flank

Sitting astride, the vaulter swings their legs forward to create momentum before swinging them back behind them and rolling onto their tummy, fully extending their legs out behind them. From here, the vaulter turns their body to the inside to take a sideways seat.

Did you know?
Vaulters compete in teams, pas-de-deux (two riders) and individually.

> **There were so many positive vibes in the vaulting team**

Vaulting horses

Any horse or pony with a calm and willing temperament can become a vaulting horse, but most often larger, wider draught breeds are used for serious competition.

Harry and Ginge, the two gorgeous horses I rode during my lessons, are both huge, with Harry standing at 18.2hh and Ginge 17.1hh!

Fancy having a go?

There are several clubs around the country offering vaulting lessons and usually, just as I did, you'll start off on a stationary barrel before trying it out on a horse. After the stationary barrel, I was fortunate enough to try some of the exercises on Woody, the mechanical horse, which prepared me for doing the same exercises on Harry and Ginge.

Check out the vaulting website to find your nearest centre **britishvaulting.org**

4 WAYS WITH
Summer
WAVES

Feel like you're at the beach with this superb summer set up

THE SET UP

What you'll need: Six poles

The arrangement: Place the poles in a zig-zag line so that the gap between the end of the poles is the same as one pole's length. For my 'route one' exercise, you may need to bring the poles closer together so the distance between them at the centre is right for your pony's stride length. Head to page 13 for my simple trot pole guide!

IN AND OUT

It's time to test our accuracy with this fun exercise. It's basically a series of small circles, changing the rein each time we go over a pole. As I head over the first pole, I'm already looking around the first circle to the second pole. I guide Joey round the circle by making sure my upper body follows the line I want to take and my outside leg is guiding him around the circle and keeping him forward. As we ride over the next pole, I ask Joey to change his bend and to circle in the opposite direction to the third pole. On each circle I focus on making sure Joey and I are both following the line of the circle by turning my shoulders and hips, and that we meet the centre of each pole at a 90-degree angle.

WIGGLY WARM UP

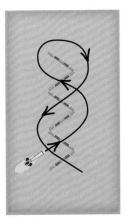

After completing my warm up for polework (see page 12) I like to walk through this pattern. It gets Joey listening to me and focusing on the poles without having to work too hard. This pattern has lots of changes of rein so I make sure Joey's responsive to my outside leg and hand as I guide him around each turn before riding straight towards each pole. 》

ROUTE ONE

This is a tricky line and I have only introduced it to Joey now that he's confident going through straight lines of poles and going over individual ones at an angle. Because he's a big horse, he can comfortably manage the 1.5 metre gap between the centre of the poles on this set up (using standard 3m poles). If I were riding this exercise with Casper I would close them up a bit to suit his shorter stride length. The idea is to ride straight through the middle of the poles so that each individual pole is on an angle as you go over it – you'll travel through the zigzag on a straight line. I'm not going to lie – the first time we tried this, Joey had a good look at what I was asking him to do! Luckily, I'd given him plenty of time to work out the question he was facing by making my turn early and riding him forward with a straight approach. As we travel down the length of poles, I look straight ahead and enjoy the fabulous feeling I get as Joey really lifts his hooves up and over the poles.

ON POINT

This is an ace way to improve your accuracy! Before you ride the line, practise riding out over a single point. It's easier if you ride from the wide end of the poles out over the point, so do this before you attempt to ride straight over the pointy end.

When I was teaching Joey to go through the very centre of the point, I rode a neat turn onto the line, giving him plenty of room to see what he needed to do. As I finished the turn, I went into sitting trot so that I could really channel his straightness before rising again one stride before the point. This way I had a nice light seat as he stepped over the poles. Once Joey was happy and confident going from the wide-open end of the poles out over the point from both directions, I used the same technique to ride straight over the pointy end first. It's a good idea to build this up over a few training sessions so that you're both feeling super-confident before you ride this serpentine movement through the points.

Start in a collected trot and make wide sweeping turns as you ride from one point to the next. It's vital that you get straight before you ride towards a point, so don't worry if the route you take is a bit loopier than the diagram!

I love this set up as it gives me so many options I can ride

MAKE A
DONKEY BOOKMARK

Never lose your place again with these
super-cute Bruno bookmarks

What you'll need:
- two colours of felt
- scissors
- PVA glue
- black marker pen
- templates on page 101
- googly eyes
- faux fur off cuts

 1 Cut out the templates on page 101. You can photocopy or trace them if you don't want to cut your yearbook.

4 With the PVA glue, stick the head onto the body. Then add the muzzle and tail.

 2 Pin each template to the felt or carefully draw around it. I've done the head, body and tail in the same colour and the muzzle in a lighter shade so that it looks like Bruno – but you can mix and match!

 5 Draw two nostrils and a mouth on the muzzle using a marker pen, and stick on the googly eyes.

 3 Using your scissors, carefully cut out all the pieces.

6 Finally cut two small pieces of the faux fur and glue them to the head and tail.

66 I normally have two or three books on the go at any time — so I love having these bookmarks to make sure I don't lose my place 99

SUPER-HAPPY
ZOOMIES

When you trust your pony to gallop across an open plain it's a seriously amazing feeling, but if you need a bit of help boosting your confidence try these tips!

Safety first

You'll definitely feel safer in the saddle knowing you've got the right protection. An approved safety helmet is an absolute must, and you might want to think about safety stirrups and a body protector, too. Plus, if you aren't being followed by your very own film crew, I'd recommend wearing high-vis so that if the worst does happen, you and your pony can be easily found.

Build up gradually

If you're lacking confidence out hacking, your feelings might not change overnight. Just as you would set yourself a goal for a jumping or dressage competition, try setting a hacking goal that you can work towards. If you'd like to gallop along the beach one day but are currently struggling to get out of the yard, book a lesson with your instructor or ask an experienced rider if you can tuck in behind them. Write down some manageable steps to help you on your way – like getting your pony used to puddles and riding in open spaces.

Know your way

If you're worried about getting lost or aren't sure what's coming around the next corner, your pony is sure to pick up on it. When you try a new route see if you can go with someone who has done the ride before, or ask your family if they'd like to go on a walk or bike ride before you head out on your pony. You can use a map or GPS, but nothing compares to the comfort you'll feel from knowing the way.

Perfect position

A good position isn't just for the arena – it's even more valuable when you're out and about. Having a secure lower leg and a strong core will really boost your confidence. All those fun games you might have played at your riding school or Pony Club were all leading up to this moment – so you can quickly regain your position if your pony is spooked or tries to head off a bit too quickly!

> **My favourite thing in the world has got to be zoomies with Casper**

Fake it

If you're struggling with your confidence a bit, it can really help to pretend to ride like someone you admire. I like to think of Felicity Collins when I'm riding – it makes me push my heels down and keep my weight back in the saddle. Give it a go – before you know it you might actually be riding like them!

Go trekking

Holiday centres specialise in taking all kinds of riders out on amazing hacks. They're experts at matching horses and riders for maximum fun and will help you remember why you wanted to go hacking in the first place. Why not see if you can get a family member to join you, too?

Practise makes perfect

No one would expect you and your pony to fly around a course of jumps that are a metre high if you haven't jumped a 40cm cross pole together, so try not to expect the equivalent out hacking. Start off with gentle walks and trots along contained bridle paths, then see if you can do a schooling session in a field. If it's going well, try a little canter – but always test your breaks before you get carried away. If you build up slowly you'll be super-zooming in no time!

PUZZLE FUN!

Silhouette stumper

See if you can put one of each pony in every row, column and quarter.

DUKE

CASPER

MICKEY

JOEY

Spot the difference

Can you spot all seven changes to this picture of me and Joey after our first ever dressage test?

Did you know?
Even though I think of myself as a showjumper, I love doing dressage with Joey and it's given me so much confidence!

Turn to page 100 for the answers!

HOW TO RIDE...
A 20 METRE CIRCLE

A 20 metre circle is one of the most common moves you'll ride when you're schooling – in fact, you probably ride them all the time without really thinking about them! But are your circles truly round? Are they the right size? And is your pony staying straight on the circle? Find out how I train for the perfect 20 metre circle.

Super straight

For many riders, the key to riding an accurate 20 metre circle is to remember that when you're riding a circle at A, you actually only touch the track three times – at A, half way between A and E, and half way between B and A. Your circle will also pass through X, which is the imaginary marker in the middle of the arena. Circles don't have corners, so from the moment you pass A you should be heading to the next point where your circle reaches the track on a curved line. Really focus on the four points of your circle and, each time you reach one of them, look up and ahead to the next one.

This Esme

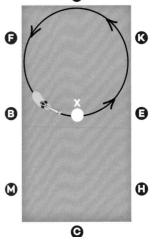

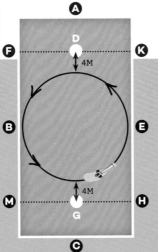

Riding a 20 metre circle at E or B is much harder than riding one at A or C as you only touch the track twice. The other two points to aim for are 4 metres in from the D and G markers as you cross the centre line. If you find it hard to visualise these points, put some cones out to help you.

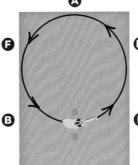

Too small

If your circle keeps ending up too small, the chances are it isn't reaching the X marker half way down the arena, or you aren't meeting the track between A and E and B and A. To help you, place four cones – each one just inside where your circle should meet the track, then ride around them for the right size circle.

Too big

If your circle is too big when you're riding a 20 metre circle from A – you really need to focus on hitting the X marker and not drifting out towards the C marker. This time, use two cones – one either side of X – so that you have a one-metre gap to ride through.

Staying straight

It seems like a really strange thing to ask – is my pony staying straight on a circle? Surely he can't be straight if he's on a circle! Well, actually he can. When I ask myself if Joey's straight when I'm on a circle what I'm really thinking about is whether his whole body is following the line of the circle. I want him to have an even bend from the tip of his nose to his tail. If his neck is curling round to the inside, but his body is fixed in a straight line, he's not straight on the circle.

3 WAYS TO SPOT A BHF
(best horsey friend)

Mickey and Duke honestly seem to have such a special connection. Here are my telltale signs ponies are besties...

1 Friendly faces

Horses communicate with body language way more than we do. The position of their ears or a slight flick of the tail gives a lot of info away about how they're feeling towards another horse. So when they approach another equine in the field their body language says a lot about whether it's a friendly approach or they want the other horse to stay away.

It's clear to see that Mickey wants to be friends with Duke. He lowers his head so as not to appear threatening and his ears are softly forwards. Horse behaviourists see this kind of friendly approach as an important measure of whether horses do share a social bond with each other.

2 Stay close to me

When two horses stay within a horse's length or two of each other for a few minutes at a time it's a good sign that they're BHFs. Some days Duke and Mickey practically try to eat the same blade of grass when they're in the field together, so I think it's safe to say they feel pretty relaxed in each other's company!

3 Super scratchies

Horses groom one another by using their teeth to scratch the mane, back and wither areas. By standing head to tail they can groom each other at the same time – but this takes trust and a mutual understanding. It also helps if you can reach the other horse's mane so I don't think Duke would be a great match for Joey unless he learns to stand up on a big box!

Not only do Mickey and Duke groom each other pretty much every day, Mickey also likes to lick Duke from time to time. I always know when he's been doing it as Duke is covered in wet patches!

Did you know?
Some people think that horses are more likely to form a friendship with a horse of the same colour.

10/10 BRIDLE FITTING

I love my Voltaire bridles, but it's not enough just to have amazing tack – it's got to fit right, too!

Headpiece

Browband

Cheek piece

Cavesson noseband

Throatlash

Bit

Reins

Quick fit checks

The noseband should sit two fingers width below the horse's cheekbone. You should be able to fit two fingers within the front of the noseband to make sure it's not too tight.

The best way of checking the tightness of the throatlash is to place a hand inside the strap. You should be able to comfortably get all four fingers in at a right angle to the horse's cheeks.

Putting on a bridle

1. Place the reins over your pony's head.

2. Ask your pony to open his mouth by carefully putting your thumb at the side of his mouth in the gap between his incisors, the front teeth used for biting, and his molars, the ones used for chewing. With his mouth open, gently slide the bit into his mouth until it rests in the space where there are no teeth.

3. Take the headpiece up and over your pony's ears so that it sits neatly on top of his head and is nicely back from his ears.

4. If your pony has a long forelock, pull it through so that it sits on top of the browband.

5. Fasten the throatlash first as this will prevent the bridle from slipping off if your pony shakes his head.

6. Finally, do up the buckle at the back of the noseband – making sure the straps sit inside the cheek pieces.

BELIEVE IT, ACHIEVE IT!

Goal setting adds a little spice to your horsey life and helps you achieve bigger and better things! Here's what to consider before you begin

You guys know me, I love setting myself challenges. There's nothing more awesome than the feeling of accomplishment that comes with achieving something new. The journey towards ticking off a goal is *sooo* satisfying, too!

If you want to achieve some horsey goals this year, it's important to set yourself up for success. Here are my tips to help you start on the right path.

1. What kind of goal?

Your goal might be to enter a dressage competition or jump a certain height, but don't limit yourself – setting goals out of the saddle are just as fun! Maybe you want to learn how to plait your pony's mane and tail, clip him yourself or become a pro at lungeing. The possibilities are endless!

2. Break it down

It's ace to dream big, but when you only focus on the end product it can feel really overwhelming. Instead, think of achieving your goal as a step-by-step process – nobody becomes perfect at something overnight, so think about the milestones you'll achieve along the way. It's much easier to work towards your goal in bite-size chunks and it'll help you measure your progress, too!

3. Get some support

It's almost impossible to learn something new all by yourself, so speak to a pro and get them involved in your goal-making process. This could mean chatting to your coach about your aims and working on them in your lessons, or getting some tips from someone at the yard who's boss-level at the skill you want to perfect.

4. Think about timescale

We've all seen those annoying moments in films where someone goes from total beginner to winning a jumping competition in like two days. We know that, in real life, it takes a lot of time and training to become a great rider – and this is something to bear in mind when you set your goal. Give yourself long enough to reach your target and don't be too hard on yourself.

5. Track your progress

I love journaling – jotting down all the things you've learnt helps you see how far you've come! You can get riding journals especially for horsey goals or use a regular notebook to summarise your training sessions.

6. Don't go it alone

Working towards a goal can be super-satisfying, but a little disheartening if you feel you're not making as much progress as you'd like. It's important to remember that everyone has setbacks, but you can overcome them with support from your coach, grown-ups at home and your yard pals. Why not all work towards a goal together to share in the highs and spur each other on through the challenges?

Top tip

YouTube is such a helpful resource when you're trying to learn something new. There's bound to be a video masterclass for you!

ADVENTURES
IN AFRICA

I literally had the trip of a lifetime on safari – I'm so excited to share it with you!

There's only one thing that can make seeing incredible wild animals in their natural environment better – and that's doing it on horseback! Horizon Horseback invited me to South Africa and Botswana for the adventure of a lifetime and it certainly didn't disappoint. From sunrise to sunset there was so much to see and do – from herding up the horses for their breakfast, to galloping flat out across the plains, hanging out with herds of zebra and tiptoeing closer to elephants. It was certainly a fortnight I'll never forget!

So worth the early start!

Herd life

Every morning the guides head out into the bush to round up the 100-strong herd of horses and bring them back over a kilometre to the lodge. One morning I was lucky enough to play an important part in this, keeping the horses in the middle section of the herd on track and making sure there were no stragglers. Cantering alongside the water's edge as the sun started to burn through the mist was so magical I'd have happily got up early every day to help with the herding!

Once all the horses are in the paddock, it's time to give them breakfast – the most important meal of the day. Around 14 horses are selected to go out on rides each morning, and they're given a full groom. The others have time to relax and chill with their friends. It honestly melts my heart to see the beautiful friendships and interactions of such a big herd.

Having a breather

Patience is key on safari

Meeting like-minded riders

> **When the horses are all tacked up, it's time to head out for the morning ride**

A dream come true

Quite literally, no two rides are the same in South Africa as you never know what you're going to see next. On one particular morning we got to see a pair of hippos with their calf enjoying a bathe in the river. It was so incredible to see these beautiful animals enjoying themselves in their natural environment. After stopping to take it all in, we headed on our way and within minutes we were enjoying a super-splashy canter as we rode past a dam.

Being on horseback meant we were able to ride close to zebra, ostrich and eland. These gentle creatures can be nervous around humans because they're prey for larger, carnivorous animals – but as horses are also flight animals they don't see them as a threat and allowed us into their space. »

Did you know?
The horses wear western or stock saddles as they're so comfy to spend a whole day riding in.

> In Botswana I got to see four of the
> big five in their natural habitat — and
> one or two smaller favourites of mine

Super-splashy canters

What a cute family!

So many stars

Time out at the waterhole

Feeling the heat

Fast and furious!

Majestic giraffes

Out in the bush

Riding for miles and miles

Amazing sunsets!

DONKEY
BUZZ

How many of these cool facts did
you know about donkeys?

Did you know?
In many parts of the world donkeys
are working animals. They're
chosen over horses for their ability
to cope with tricky terrain.

Did you know?
Donkeys can live for
more than 50 years.

Did you know?
They have amazing memories
and seem to be able to recognise
other donkeys they haven't seen
for more than 20 years.

Did you know?
Their big ears actually help them to
hear. In their natural environment,
donkey herds wander over huge areas
and their large ears help them to hear
herd mates over long distances.

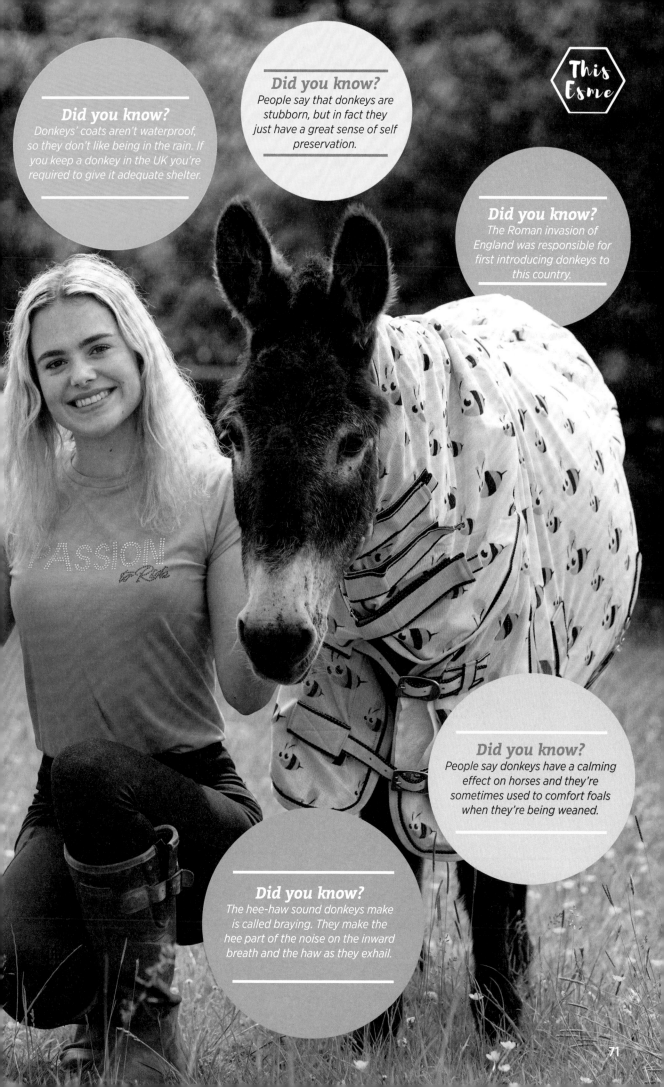

Did you know?
Donkeys' coats aren't waterproof, so they don't like being in the rain. If you keep a donkey in the UK you're required to give it adequate shelter.

Did you know?
People say that donkeys are stubborn, but in fact they just have a great sense of self preservation.

Did you know?
The Roman invasion of England was responsible for first introducing donkeys to this country.

Did you know?
People say donkeys have a calming effect on horses and they're sometimes used to comfort foals when they're being weaned.

Did you know?
The hee-haw sound donkeys make is called braying. They make the hee part of the noise on the inward breath and the haw as they exhail.

THE HOLISTIC
HOUSE

Autumn

Exercise body and mind with the house challenge!

> "This is a great set up if you only have a few poles as you can ride lots of different lines through it!"

THE SET UP

What you'll need: 6 poles

The arrangement: Place four poles in a square in the centre of the arena. Then place two more poles to form a triangle with the pole at the top of your square.

IN AND OUT

This is a super-easy way to start a polework session after warming up. I simply ride Joey into the middle of the house over one pole and out over the other side. Once Joey has stepped out over the second pole, I keep him straight for two or three strides and then turn in alternate directions each time I ride through to make sure he's listening to me. If I want to add in an extra dimension to this line, I ask Joey to make a transition within the two poles. This can either be walk to trot, or for a bigger challenge trot-halt-trot.

DIAGONAL LINES

Another way you can use this set up is to ride diagonal lines through the square part of the house. Start by riding one line at a time. I make sure Joey's straight before I approach the first corner and then look up and ahead as I ride through the box and out the other side. If Joey tries to wriggle to either side I close my leg around his sides to correct him. Once he's got the hang

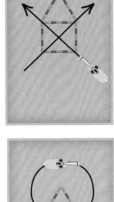

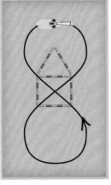

of it I move on to riding the diagonal lines as part of a figure of eight which really makes Joey think about what he's doing. »

STRAIGHT TO IT

The direct route is to ride in through the house and out through the roof. Beginning in walk, I ride Joey forward through the very middle of the first pole, over the next pole and then out through the point. I try to keep him straight by keeping my rein contact even and my legs gently 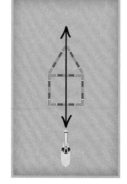 wrapped around his sides. Once I've ridden him through the set up from both reins in walk, I pick up trot.

It's a bit trickier to stay straight in trot, so I sometimes sit for a couple of strides as I come off the corner to set us up on the perfect line. I then rise to the trot as we get close to the first pole. As we travel through the house, I use my legs to make sure Joey maintains a nice forward rhythm. The first time I rode Joey out of the roof in trot, he wasn't quite sure what he was being asked to do so he did a tiny leap out over the poles!

THROUGH THE ROOF

It's so much harder to ride the direct route going the other way as you need to be super accurate when you ask your pony to step in through the point of the roof. I think it's a great test of straightness, though, and you guys know how much I love a challenge! Going back into walk, I make a neat turn towards the point of the roof using my outside leg to guide Joey. Once we're straight I choose a point on the horizon and try not to take my eyes off it. This helps me to guide Joey directly through the middle and stops me from looking down at the poles. With even aids, Joey should stay straight – but if I need to make a slight adjustment, I close the leg aid on the side he's drifting to and ride forward.

Once we mastered this trickier line in walk I pick up trot and try to ride it in the same way – looking at the same point on the horizon and with everything nice and even.

You can also ride through the top of
this set up on a circle – check out
page 95 to find out how

This
Esme

WINTER CARE
ROUTINE

*At this time of year there are a few little extra things I like
to do to make sure my horses love winter as much as I do*

FOOT PERFECT

People always say 'no foot no horse' and this time of year it's especially important to keep a really close eye on their feet. I pick out all the equines hooves every morning and evening – and in between if I'm riding! With all the mud and damp conditions, I look to see if their shoes are coming loose as they can get sucked off in deep mud – especially if the horses are messing around. I also check on the health of their sole and frog – looking for any signs of thrush.

Did you know?
Thrush is a bacterial infection that often starts in the frog clefts. It's caused by standing in deep mud, dirty bedding or very wet grass. You can often smell thrush before you see it as it has a disgusting smelly discharge.

SNUG AS A BUG

In the winter months, I like to clip Joey and Casper so they don't get too hot and sweaty when I ride them. This means they need to wear a rug when it's chilly so they don't get cold. During the day I use a turnout rug which is both warm and waterproof – as an added bonus it helps to keep them clean, too! At night, both horses wear stable rugs which make sure they stay cosy.

Duke and Mickey are native types and often don't need to wear rugs no matter what the weather. I like to keep a close eye on Mickey because he's older – it's important he's maintaining his weight and not burning too many calories just to keep warm.

HUNGRY HORSES

When the grass is poor and offers little nutritional value, I put haylage nets out for the horses so they have plenty of forage to eat. Horses need to eat around 2–2.5% of their bodyweight every day to maintain healthy digestion – so when there's little food about it's important to supplement the grass with either hay or haylage. When horses get cold they can use up to 80% of their energy keeping warm, so it's vital they have the right balance of food and warmth.

Even though Casper, Mickey, Joey and Duke are all good friends, I always put out more haynets than horses to stop them from squabbling over food. It also keeps them moving around the field which is good for their digestion and well-being.

FROZEN

If temperatures drop below freezing, I have to check all the water troughs and break through any ice so that the horses are always able to drink. Some horses can be hesitant to drink very cold water, so if I'm worried about any of them I add some warm water to their bucket to take off the chill. Other people suggest adding apple juice to their water to tempt them – tasty!

MUD BATH

During the winter months some horses suffer from mud fever which is a bacterial infection that occurs when horses' skin is weakened by wet and muddy conditions and causes scabs and lesions on the leg. I make sure my horses aren't suffering by checking their legs carefully each time I groom them. If you're ever worried about mud fever, it's best to speak to your pony's vet.

HOW TO RIDE...

A CHANGE OF TROT DIAGONAL

Trot diagonals can be tricky to master at first, but once you know how, there'll be no stopping you. Read on to discover how I check I'm on the correct trot diagonal

Two-beat trot

Your pony's trot is a two-beat pace, which is why you can rise up and down to it in balance. He moves his legs in diagonal pairs – the inside foreleg and outside hindleg move together and then the outside foreleg and inside hindleg do the same.

On a corner or circle, most of your pony's weight will be carried on his inside hindleg because he uses it to step underneath his body. You can make his job easier by rising as his outside foreleg is forwards, so your weight will be off his back at that moment.

Sounds complicated? Don't panic, it's really not. The simple way to check you're on the correct diagonal is to glance down at your pony's outside foreleg – the one nearest the track. You'll clearly see his shoulder move forward and back as he works in diagonal pairs, and you need to be in the rising stage of the trot as his outside shoulder moves forward and sitting as it comes back.

Changing the rein

When you change the rein from left to right or right to left you'll also need to change your trot diagonal, otherwise you'll be on the wrong diagonal when you start going in the new direction. You can change your trot diagonal anywhere you like before you've changed the rein, but it looks neater if it's done at the halfway stage. For example, if you're changing the rein across the long diagonal KXM, make your change of trot diagonal over X.

Did you know?

It's a good idea to change your trot diagonal regularly out hacking because staying on the same diagonal could make your pony become one-sided and stiffer on one rein.

What to do

It's super easy to change your trot diagonal – you just sit to the trot for two beats instead of one. As I change direction with Joey, I sit for two beats – up, down, down, up – then glance down at his new outside leg to double check I've got it right. I don't need to lean over to check, just a little glance with the eyes, keeping my head up so I don't unbalance Joey and lose the trot rhythm.

Test your feel

As you get to grips with trot diagonals, you'll start to feel when it's right rather than having to glance down to check. A great way to put this to the test is to ask a friend or your instructor to watch while you tell them whether you think you're correct or not – without looking down. The more you do this, the better you'll become.

HAVE A GO AT...
SIDE SADDLE

You guys know that I've always wanted to give side saddle a proper try, so I jumped at the chance of learning this sophisticated skill

OFF YOUR HEAD

Side saddles are completely unlike any saddle I've ever ridden in. They have two, hook-like projections mounted on the left-hand side of the saddle. The top one is called the fixed head and the one below it is called the leaping head. The other big difference is that side saddles have just one stirrup. Traditionally ladies would each keep their own stirrup and would attach it to the saddle of the horse they were about to get on – so that it was always the correct length for them – and take it away with them at the end of the ride, too.

Side saddles also have an extra girth. The main girth goes from one side to the other just like a traditional saddle. The second girth is fastened over this and goes from the normal girthing area on the left-hand side of the saddle to the back of the saddle on the right-hand side. This is called a balance strap and its job is to counter the weight of the rider, which falls mostly on the left-hand side.

SITTING PRETTY

From behind, riders who are riding aside should look exactly the same as those riding astride – centred in the saddle. The left leg sits below the leaping head and is used in the same way as it would if you were riding astride. The right leg goes around the fixed head and then hangs down on the left hand side of the horse's shoulder. Unlike traditional riding, you point the toe of the right leg down towards the ground. This helps you to grip onto the fixed head if you need to. The left thigh should sit loosely under the leaping head, but if you need to grip on for any reason, pushing this leg up into the leaping head and clamping your right leg down on the fixed head will make it pretty hard for you to fall off – although I did manage it going over a jump!

> **I was aiming for elegant lady, but I'll admit I did look a little bit like the fat controller**

Aside not astride

We all know the aids for walk, trot and canter when you're sitting astride a horse, but how do you communicate with a horse using just one leg? Side saddle riders use a crop on the right-hand side to replicate the aids they give the horse with their left leg. If you use your left leg to ask the horse to go forward, you must also place the crop on the horse's right side to gently encourage him forwards. This felt really strange to begin with.

Your rein aids should be exactly the same as when you ride astride, but you do really need to concentrate on keeping your shoulders square on to the horse and not twisting through your middle. When you're starting out it's easier to ride on the right rein so that your legs are on the outside of your circle. When you move on to the left rein and your legs are on the inside of your circle it feels as though you might just slide off the side of the saddle as you look to the inside. »

Not hot to trot

It's not particularly comfortable to trot when you're riding aside. For one thing, you have to sit to the trot because you can't rise with just the one stirrup. I found myself using the emergency grip around the fixed and leaping heads quite a bit! After a while I got the hang of it, but cantering side saddle is *sooo* much more fun!

Jump to it

Keen to take it to the next level, I had a little jump riding side saddle, which was amazing! Essentially you approach the fence in the same way as you would when you're jumping normally, but as you go over the fence you need to think about your left shoulder folding forwards and down towards your horse's right ear. It's also a good idea to grip your legs around the fixed and leaping heads and make sure your right toe is pointing down. I had so much fun jumping side saddle and when I did slip off the side I was lucky enough to land on my feet!

Dressed for Downton

Obviously you can't ride side saddle without wanting to dress up! Here I'm wearing a beautiful navy habit, which has an elegant skirt. I'm also wearing a hunting stock, waistcoat and this incredible top hat. You know me, I didn't actually ride in the top hat as it wouldn't offer any real protection in a fall, but it was fun to try it on!

Elegant equitation

My final task of the day was to learn and ride an equitation test on Toby. It's quite like a dressage test with lots of circles, transitions and movements to remember – but Toby was a total legend and made it easy for me.

SMILE!

Check out my top tips for taking Instagram perfect pics every time

This Esme

Beware of your background

Before you get your camera out, take a look around you. Is there a big mess on the yard? Is there someone poo-picking in the field behind you? Try to look for a clean background that lets your pony be the centre of attention, or a beautiful scene that adds to the mood of your shot – perhaps bluebell woods or autumn leaves. Look at the mess behind me in the shot above! The jump wing makes it look like I've got an orange balanced on my head!

Ears forward

All horses look *sooo* much cuter when they have their ears pricked and are interested in what's going on around them. Because I photograph my horses a lot I have a few tricks up my sleeve to make sure they've got their ears forward when I need them to. My top three ways of doing this are:

1. Waving or scrunching paper.
2. Playing the sound of other horses on my phone (this is Joey's favourite).
3. If all else fails... shake the famous treat tin!

No slouching

When you're trying to make your pony look super-smart for a photo you need to make sure he's standing up properly. Here Mickey's resting one leg and he's half asleep – certainly not his best look! Walk your pony on for a few steps and then ask him for a square halt so that you can see how lovely he really is.

Clever crops

If you're photographing the whole of your pony it's important to make sure you get all of him in. There's nothing worse than a hoof or half a tail being accidentally missed out of the picture. However... sometimes it's great to get up close and personal with your fave pony and try out some super-cropped images. Look for a special detail that you'd like to be the focus of your image and then experiment with a few different angles where you crop right in on that detail. Some people aren't all that keen on horses with blue eyes, but to me Mickey's eyes are so beautiful. They're clear and blue and because of his sensitivity to the sun you don't always get to see how special they are. I just love this image with the contrast of the dark stable and his cream coat, which really makes the beautiful blue of his eyes pop!

JUMP-OFF
— LIKE A BOSS —

Want to ace your next jump-off?
Here are my top tips

If you've never been in a jump-off before then oh my goodness, you're in for a treat! The jump-off is the second round of a showjumping competition for riders who were lucky enough to go clear in the first. Its purpose? To decide who wins. A shortened version of the course you jumped initially, and usually a hole or two higher, it's the ultimate test of speed and accuracy – because it's ridden against the clock!

To ride your best-ever jump-off, you need to be super-focused, in a great rhythm and have your route all planned out. If you're a first-timer or want to step up your performance, here are my favourite jump-off tactics.

1 Look before you leap

When you walk the jump-off course you need to plan your route carefully. There are likely to be obstacles in your way that you must decide whether you'll ride around – taking longer – or cut inside – risking a tight turn into the next fence. Think about the types of fences in the course – upright planks for example need a steady approach to make sure your pony doesn't knock them, whereas you might get away with galloping to an oxer. The skill in planning an ace jump-off is knowing your pony so well you make the right decision for his strengths and weaknesses.

2 Get in the zone

You'll want to get back in the collecting ring to loosen your pony up and get him listening ready for the jump-off. While the aim is to get round in the least possible time, speeding around the collecting ring and popping jump after jump isn't the best way to prepare your pony – it's not safe, you might tire him out, and he could get too excitable. I find riding lots of transitions is great for getting your pony to concentrate. The best part is that it works for horses who tend to get carried away, like Joey, and also revvs up a steadier sort like Casper!

Top tip

If you're not first to jump, it's a great idea to watch one or two other riders go in the jump-off before you.

Did you know?
It's more important to go clear than quickly – first place goes to the fastest clear round.

3 Fast not furious

Seriously guys, a quick time is great but galloping at full speed and slamming on the brakes for the turns isn't the way to do it! Every superstar rider I've spoken to always says the same thing – focus on keeping a positive, even rhythm and stick to your route. The transitions you did in your warm-up will help keep your pony in front of your leg, so focus on maintaining that energy without letting him get too fast or strong! »

If you're not first to jump, it's a great idea to watch one or two other riders jump before you

4 Ahead of the game

Don't wait for your pony to land before you look to your next fence – do it as he's taking off to jump the one before. Why? Because this will make you shift your weight and signal to your pony which canter lead he needs to land on and will ensure he keeps as balanced as possible throughout your winning round.

Top tip

While in an ideal world you'd gallop around the jump-off at a blistering pace with the tightest of time-saving turns, remember to ride the pony you've got. You can work towards riding the round of your dreams with your coach, it'll soon be a reality!

5 Prepare for your turns

Has your instructor ever told you your pony's going around a corner like a motorbike? It means you're going too fast and he's drifting. Prepare him for all your turns with a little squeeze on the rein and use your outside leg to guide him round, rather than pulling him with your inside rein. Most importantly, look where you're going as this will help your pony, too!

6 Confidence is key

If you or your pony don't feel up to reaching top speed, then it's absolutely cool to ride your round at a sensible pace that'll boost your confidence. It's easy to put pressure on yourself to go for the win, but this can lead to confidence-slashing mistakes if you're not ready. My advice? Go for the route that will be the most fun to ride at your own pace, and as you and your pony gain experience you'll be able to tackle tougher routes with ease. Plus, you never know – sometimes going clear is all it takes to win!

Top tip

The order you'll jump is usually decided by who went fastest in the first round, so make sure you know when it will be your turn to go.

7 Start small

If you aren't used to jumping your pony at speed it's a great idea to step down a height so that you can both get your confidence up. Jumping smaller fences gives you more room to make a small mistake and get away with it while you're still polishing off your jumping skills. Casper loves to jump the second round quickly as he tends to get more and more buzzy the more he jumps – but whatever happens, whether we're fast or slow, I like to reward him with some neck scratchies or a special treat when he's done a fab job.

"Any stress melts away when I spend quality time with the donkeys"

MAKE HORSEY
PHOTO LETTERS

I love surrounding myself with pictures of my horses – why not make your own initial and include your fave ponies, too?

What you'll need:
- 3D box photo frame
- photos or printouts of your fave images
- scissors
- card
- glue
- small copper screw-in rings
- picture wire or string
- mini wooden pegs or bull dog clips
- confetti

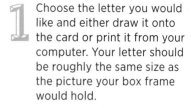

1 Choose the letter you would like and either draw it onto the card or print it from your computer. Your letter should be roughly the same size as the picture your box frame would hold.

2 Using your photos, cut sections out and glue them onto the card to completely cover your letter. Try to include as many different images as you can and avoid having to chop people's heads off!

3 Screw one small copper ring on each side of your 3D frame approximately 40mm from the top.

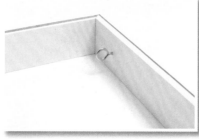

4 Tie the picture wire or string from one copper ring to the other, then use your mini wooden pegs to clip your photo letter on.

5 Finally add some confetti to the bottom of your box frame before slotting the back of the frame into place.

WINTER WORKOUT WITH POLES

This Christmas tree set up is a fantastic, fun, festive challenge!

THE SET UP

What you'll need: 8 poles

The arrangement: Start by building a triangle of poles in the middle of your arena. Build a second triangle at the top of the first one. Then add two guide poles, at least 1m apart, at the bottom of the first triangle.

TOP OF THE TREE

This exercise is trickier than it looks as you need to be really accurate – but it's so beneficial and the feeling you get when your horse connects and lifts his shoulder over the poles is immense! I pick up trot and ride a 10m circle at the top of the Christmas tree. To get the right stride length for Casper, I need to make sure the arc of my circle goes over the second coloured section of the pole as we enter and exit the triangle. If your pony is smaller striding than Casper you will need to ride your circle closer to the point of the triangle, and if he's longer striding ride a larger circle so that you're entering and exiting the circle closer to the middle of the poles.

I find that with this exercise, more than any, it's *sooo* important to look where I'm going. If I don't concentrate on the shape of my circle, it's easy for Casper to drift out and then we miss our exit stride. But looking around the circle, keeping my hips and shoulders following the line I want to take and using my outside leg to keep us on track, Casper trots in and out with ease and really uses his shoulders as he steps around and up over the poles. »

CHRISTMAS TREE CHALLENGE

Once I've done my normal polework warm up with Casper, he's ready to rock the Christmas tree vibe. This exercise is a little trickier to set up than some of the others, and it does need a lot of poles – but it's *sooo* worth it. It offers lots of variety for your pony – and it looks great, too. The first line I'm going to ride is the simplest because the guide poles help to keep Casper straight and set us up nicely for the two triangles we'll need to ride out through. In a forward working trot, I turn towards the very middle of the first triangle – making sure I look ahead and not down at the poles. As we reach the guide poles I keep my leg on to make sure Casper feels confident about the exercise. As he steps over the first pole I use soft hands to allow him to use his back and neck.

As we continue to the first point, I keep my leg on and channel Casper with my reins to keep him straight. As he steps out over the last point, I ride away positively and give him a little pat. I ride this line a few times off each rein before giving him a little break.

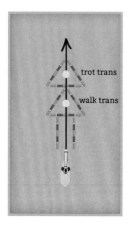

TROT WALK TROT

Using the same line as the first exercise, I ride Casper through the guide poles and into the first triangle in trot. Once I feel him step over the pole, I ask him forwards into walk. Keeping the impulsion we walk over the second pole, then I ask for an upwards transition to trot before heading out over the final point at the top of the Christmas tree. If you're not feeling quite ready to ride the two transitions within the exercise, try walking in over the first two poles and then asking your pony to trot out over the final point.

ON POINT

This time I'm taking the trickiest line through this set up. I turn Casper straight towards the very middle of the top of the Christmas tree. Sitting for a few strides helps ensure Casper is straight all the way through his body – I'm looking ahead and up through his ears, making sure his head, neck and shoulders are straight and his hindquarters are following on in a straight line, too. Of course it's no good making sure Casper's straight if I'm not! My weight needs to be spread evenly in both stirrups, I need even pressure down my reins and my hips and shoulders should be straight as well. Once we're all set, I pick up rising trot and then it's really just a case of keeping Casper in that straight channel between leg and hand as we head down the line of poles. After we make it out over the final pole, I ride positively away through the guide poles, staying straight for another five or six strides. Great job Caspie!

Top tip

If you're not used to guide poles, set up two poles 1.5 metres apart and practise with these before attempting the full exercise.

PUZZLE FUN

WORDSEARCH

Can you find all the words hidden in this grid?

```
C P D N A L E O T S N U K A R
R F T O I O N J N Y E O L T
U E C A O Z M O S M N S I U
S Z E B R A M X U N T T P L
T F B F V U T S M O M R E S
D T U S S A I O A I B I S T
P T B E B R O S T F F C D N
Q B D V A Q D T O S Y H J A
O H I F D T M O P A O C I H
U F A B D R A P O E L I S P
S S D E P Y F S P Q O S Y E
Z N T E S N U S P E P I T L
R D F T H S O G I R A F F E
C P H M O R P U H W U G S L
```

- ⬡ Safari
- ⬡ Ostrich
- ⬡ Giraffe
- ⬡ Eland
- ⬡ Lion
- ⬡ Leopard
- ⬡ Zebra
- ⬡ Elephant
- ⬡ Hippopotamus
- ⬡ Sunset

Turn to page 100 for the answers!

"There's no better way to explore the world than by horseback"

ANSWERS & TEMPLATES

Find all the answers and things you need here!

PAGE 56
SILHOUETTE STUMPER

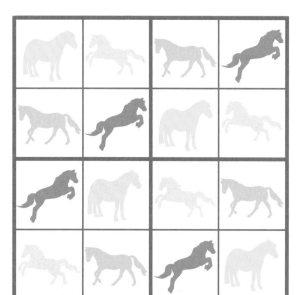

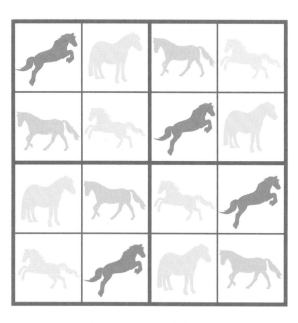

PAGE 57
SPOT THE DIFFERENCE

PAGE 98
WORDSEARCH

```
C P D N A L E O T S N U K A
R F T O I O N J N Y E O L T
U E C A O Z M O S M N S I U
S Z E B R A M X U N T T P L
T F B F V U T S M O M R E S
D T U S S A I O A I B I S T
P T B E B R O S T F F C D N
Q B D V A Q D T O S Y H J A
O H I F D T M O P A O C I H
U F A B D R A P O E L I S P
S S D E P Y F S P Q O S Y E
Z N T E S N U S P E P I T L
R D F T H S O G I R A F F E
C P H M O R P U H W U G S L
```

This
Esme

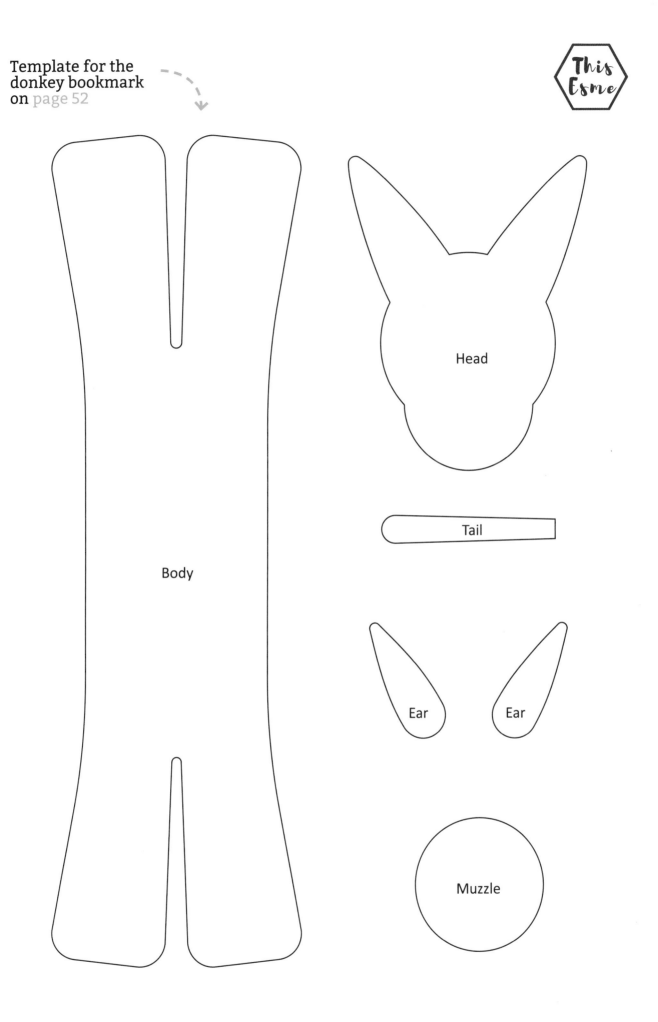

Body

Head

Tail

Ear

Ear

Muzzle